Designed in the USA
Free coloring pages at Five-44.com

PLEASE.
JUST.
STOP.

I WASN'T DOING ANYTHING

CAN I HAVE A
COOKIE?

It's 6:27 a.m. No, have some fruit.

Why is this sticky?

I
don't
know

MOMMY!?!

I'LL BE
THERE IN
A MINUTE!

Can I have a snack?

DIDN'T WE JUST HAVE LUNCH?!

PLEASE DO NOT PUT THAT IN YOUR MOUTH!

It wasn't in my mouth. It was on my chin.

Drink Some
Water

Don't
throw
that!

DID YOU BRUSH YOUR TEETH?

YES...TODAY? NO.

GET YOUR
FOOT OFF
OF THERE

OK!
JEEZ
LOUISE

DON'T LICK THAT!

ME?!?

SIT ON YOUR BUTT

Don't Put
Your Feet
On The
Walls

GET
THAT
OUT OF
YOUR
NOSE

THIS?

LOOK WHERE YOU ARE GOING

COME HERE PLEASE!

LET ME SEE

DON'T PUT
YOUR FACE
ON THAT!

I LOVE YOU

YEAH

WHY IS THIS WET ?

WOW, THAT IS GROSS

Did you
wash your
hands?

...WITH
SOAP?

Don't
eat
that!

PUT THAT
DOWN!

PLEASE,
DO NOT SIT
ON THAT

Hands
Together

Where are your shoes?

Mom, where are you?

YOU NEED A HAT

THAT IS
YUCKY!

WHERE IS YOUR
OTHER SOCK?!?

I HAVE
NO IDEA

GET
DOWN!

Mom,
I Love
You